TALES FROM AMERICANA

The Wendigo

BY MARLEY RICHMOND

CONTENT CONSULTANT
SHAAWANO URAN, PhD
ASSOCIATE PROFESSOR
INDIGENOUS STUDIES
BEMIDJI STATE UNIVERSITY

Kids Core
An Imprint of Abdo Publishing
abdobooks.com

abdobooks.com

Printed in the United States of America, North Mankato, Minnesota.
102023
012024

THIS BOOK CONTAINS RECYCLED MATERIALS

Cover Photo: Sunshower Shots/Adobe Stock
Interior Photos: Shutterstock Images, 4–5, 15, 20–21, 26, 28 (top), 28 (bottom); Old Images/Alamy, 6; Jessie Wardarski/AP Images, 8; Red Line Editorial, 10; Joe Amon/The Denver Post/Getty Images, 12–13, 29 (bottom); Ground Picture/Shutterstock Images, 17, 29 (top); Matthew Corrigan/Alamy, 18; Daniel Eskridge/Shutterstock Images, 22; Rena Schild/Shutterstock Images, 25

Editor: Angela Lim
Series Designer: Katharine Hale

Library of Congress Control Number: 2023939678

Publisher's Cataloging-in-Publication Data

Names: Richmond, Marley, author.
Title: The Wendigo / by Marley Richmond
Description: Minneapolis, Minnesota: Abdo Publishing, 2024 | Series: Tales from Americana | Includes online resources and index.
Identifiers: ISBN 9781098292898 (lib. bdg.) | ISBN 9798384910831 (ebook)
Subjects: LCSH: Windigos--Juvenile literature. | Monsters--Juvenile literature. | Animals, Mythical--Juvenile literature. | Folklore--Juvenile literature. | Cryptozoology--Juvenile literature.
Classification: DDC 398.24--dc23

CONTENTS

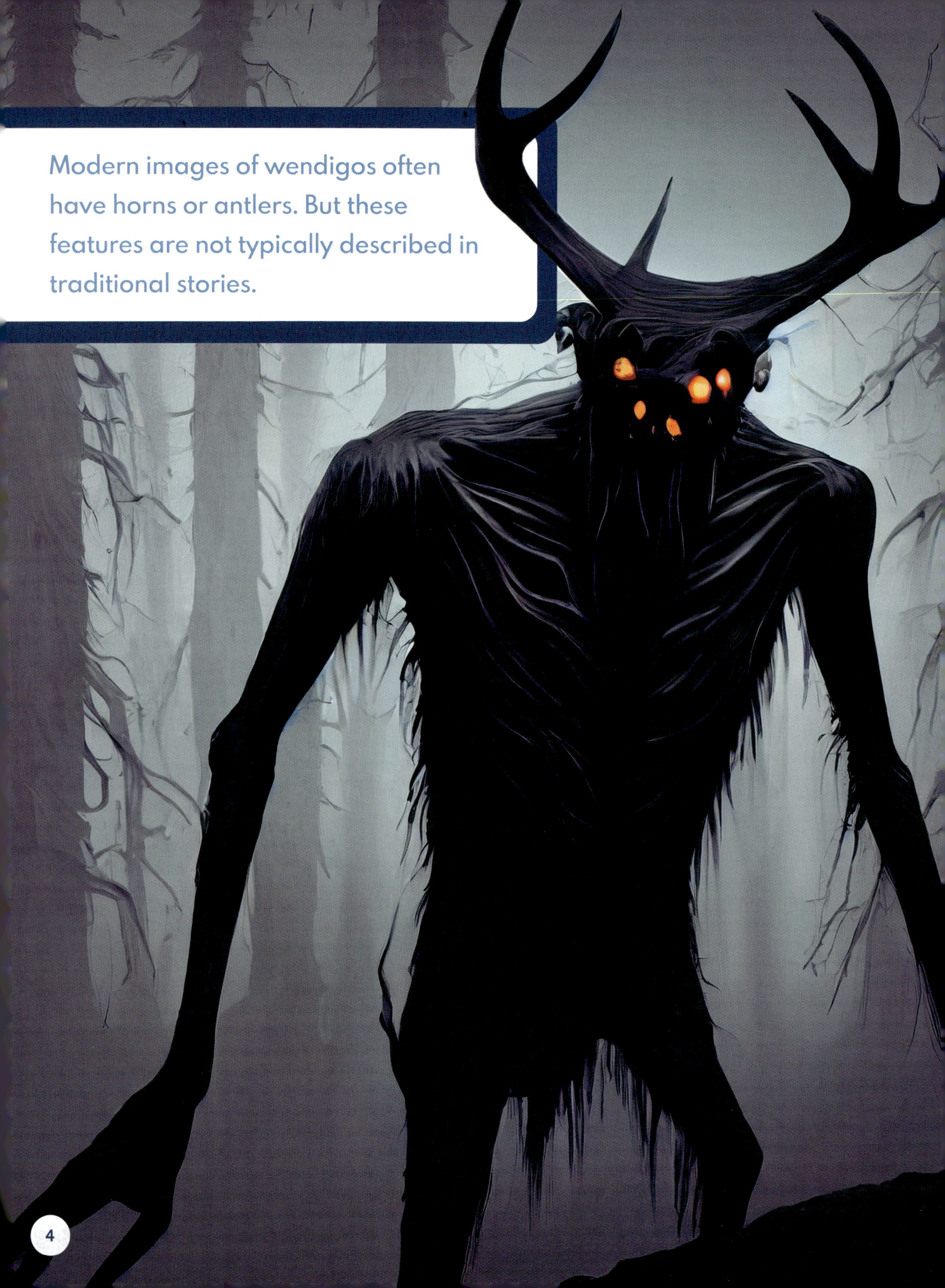

Modern images of wendigos often have horns or antlers. But these features are not typically described in traditional stories.

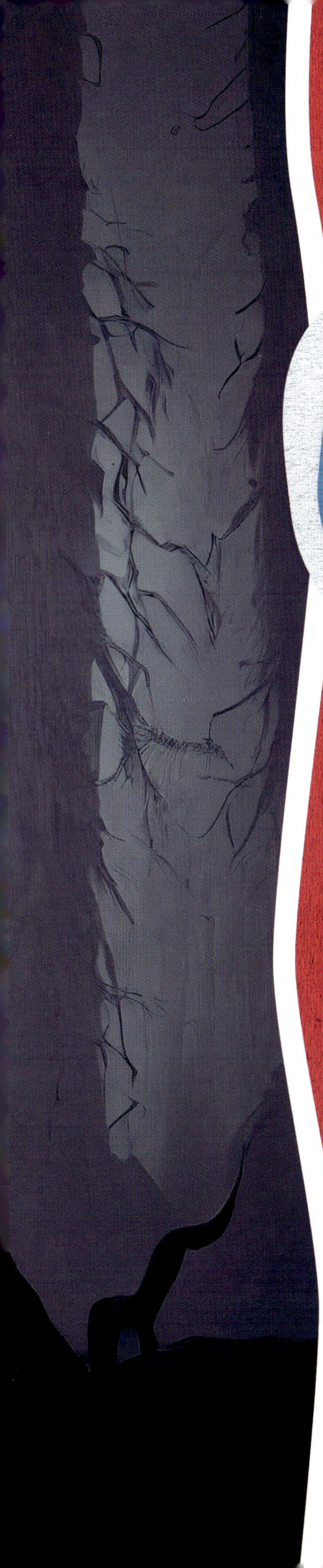

CHAPTER 1

A Monstrous Hunger

Many years ago, the people of Nipissing First Nation were preparing for winter. They had spent the summer gathering food. They had berries and dried meat. They stored corn and wild rice.

Great Lakes American Indians have traditionally gone ice fishing to get food during the winter.

They would try to hunt for food during the winter months. But there would be few animals. People knew that food might run low. A person could not be selfish. Otherwise, there might not be enough food for everyone.

That winter, the food started to run out. There was a man who wanted more than his share. His greed caused him to grow. He became six times taller than other men. And he was hungrier than ever before.

The man thought about the animals in the forest. But they didn't sound good to eat. He ran through the trees on his long legs. Soon, he found a village. When the villagers saw him, they believed he was a monster. Many of them died of fright. The man was so hungry. He began to eat the dead villagers. But the more he ate, the bigger and hungrier he became. He would never be full. The man had become a wendigo.

One villager had been away from home when the wendigo arrived. He returned and saw what the wendigo had done. He wanted revenge. The man chased the wendigo. When he finally caught it, he killed the creature that had eaten his family.

Storing food such as wild rice was once necessary to survive the winter. Wild rice is still an important crop for the Ojibwe and many other Great Lakes nations.

Beware the Wendigo

The people of Nipissing First Nation are not the only American Indian people who have stories about wendigos. Other nations in the Algonquian language family tell tales of these creatures. These nations include the Ojibwe, Potawatomi, Métis, Cree, and others. They are located in Canada and the Northeast and Great Lakes regions of the United States. People of these nations consider the wendigo to be a manitou, or spirit.

The Meaning of Wendigo

The wendigo's name has many spellings. Depending on the language, this creature might be called *weendigo*, *windigo*, or *witiko*. There are many ways to translate *wendigo*. Some people say it means "fool." Others say it means "**cannibal**." Or the name might come from the Algonquian phrase *ween dagoh*, meaning "selfish."

Students at the Arapaho School on the Wind River Reservation in Wyoming celebrate their culture and language.

CHAPTER 2

Wendigo Stories

Tales of the wendigo have been told for hundreds of years. These stories are still told by Algonquian-speaking nations today. Wendigo stories have been passed down for a purpose.

In some stories, the wendigo is a monster in the woods. But many stories tell of a human transforming into a wendigo. These tales warn listeners to be good people. Otherwise, they may become monsters.

Becoming a Wendigo

The most common cause for becoming a wendigo was being a **cannibal**. Harsh winters

Spiritual Balance

Mino-bimaadiziwin is an Ojibwe spiritual belief. It is the idea of living a balanced life. Respecting spiritual powers is part of this balance. So is respecting people, animals, plants, and all of nature. Many wendigo stories are about losing this balance by not respecting others.

Cannibalism is common in the animal kingdom. Praying mantises, for example, are cannibals.

could cause food supplies to run low. A starving person might eat another human being to stay alive. This was a terrible thing to do. Eating human flesh showed that a person valued his or her own life above someone else's.

The act was so selfish that it could turn someone into a wendigo. Wendigo stories warn people that they must care for one another. People must act as a community, not just as individuals.

Dreams play an important role in many Algonquian-language cultures. Even having a dream about becoming a wendigo could cause a person to transform in real life. A wendigo spirit could trick people while they slept.

An **elder** may be able to curse someone with bad luck. This can lead to starvation. Over time, that person might become a wendigo.

Defeating a Wendigo

In some stories, people are able to cure wendigos. People believed that wendigos

Many American Indian cultures believe in the importance of dreams. In some stories, the power of dreams could change a person into a wendigo.

had hearts made of ice. Drinking hot, liquid animal fat was thought to melt a wendigo's heart. Coughing up ice was a sign that the cure had worked.

Wendigos are sometimes described as being very thin and having glowing eyes.

Potawatomi writer Robin Wall Kimmerer told a wendigo tale. In the story, a brave woman decided to share tea with a wendigo. By sharing what she had, the woman cured the selfishness of the creature. But not all wendigos could be cured. In many stories, wendigos were killed to protect the community.

Further Evidence

Visit the website below. Does it give any new evidence about the wendigo to support Chapter Two?

Windigo

abdocorelibrary.com/wendigo

Stories about wendigos often warn against selfishness.

CHAPTER 3

The Modern Wendigo

Today, wendigos are a part of American Indian stories. They are also seen in pop culture. However, some uses of wendigos in movies and comics are disrespectful. It can be harmful when creators take pieces of cultures that are not their own.

Wendigo stories tell about the importance of community and helping others.

In the original stories, the wendigo warns people to think about others. It reminds people to share what they have.

Primary Source

Basil Johnston wrote a book called *The Manitous* about the spirits of the Ojibwe world. He said modern wendigos are the people and machines that cut down forests. He wrote:

> These mechanical [wendigos] gutted and [ruined] the forest, leaving death, destruction, and ugliness.

Source: Basil Johnston. *The Manitous: The Spiritual World of the Ojibway*. Minnesota Historical Society Press, 2001, p. 236.

Comparing Texts

Think about the quote. Does it support the information in this chapter? Or does it give a different perspective? Explain how in a few sentences.

Legendary Facts

A wendigo is a giant, humanlike creature that eats human flesh.

Wendigos are a symbol of selfishness and greed.

A human can become a wendigo through cannibalism, dreams, or a curse.

Wendigo stories tell about the importance of community and helping others.

Glossary

cannibal
a creature that eats its own kind, such as a person who eats human flesh

colonizers
people who establish a settlement, often forcing out the people who first lived in the region

elder
an older, wiser member of an American Indian community who is respected by other community members

hoard
to gather and store away a large supply

symbol
a thing that stands for or represents something else

Online Resources

To learn more about wendigos, Algonquian cultures, and legends, visit our free resource websites below.

Core Library CONNECTION
FREE! COMMON CORE MULTIMEDIA RESOURCES

Visit **abdocorelibrary.com** or scan this QR code for free Common Core resources for teachers and students, including vetted activities, multimedia, and booklinks, for deeper subject comprehension.

Booklinks NONFICTION NETWORK
FREE! ONLINE NONFICTION RESOURCES

Visit **abdobooklinks.com** or scan this QR code for free additional online weblinks for further learning. These links are routinely monitored and updated to provide the most current information available.

Learn More

Krensky, Stephen. *The Book of Mythical Beasts and Magical Creatures*. DK, 2020.

SaSuWeh Jones, Dan. *Living Ghosts and Mischievous Monsters*. Scholastic, 2021.

Index

About the Author

Marley Richmond is a children's book editor and author. She lives in Minnesota with her cat, Bean.